7 of the Holy Spirit

by
Fr Richard Conrad OP

All booklets are published thanks to the generous support of the members of the Catholic Truth Society

CATHOLIC TRUTH SOCIETY
PUBLISHERS TO THE HOLY SEE

Contents

Introduction

The Spirit of the seven gifts is called down on us when we are confirmed

Maybe you are preparing for Confirmation, and are wondering what God will give you through this Sacrament. Maybe you have been confirmed already, and are wondering what God gave you.

When we are confirmed, the Bishop, or the priest he has delegated, anoints our forehead with Chrism, perfumed oil consecrated by the Bishop just before Easter. He says, "Be sealed with the Gift of the Holy Spirit." The Holy Spirit anointed Jesus the Messiah. In Confirmation, He is sent to anoint us. Through the Spirit, God the Father seals us, marks us out as belonging to Him in a new way. In Baptism, God the Father says to us, "You are mine." In Confirmation, He says the same thing, with new depth and urgency. So we start a new stage in our journey with Jesus.

If we are to press ahead on this journey, what resources can we draw on? It would be better to ask: Who can we rely on? Before he anoints us, the Bishop stretches out his hands over us, and calls down the Holy

Spirit. Before 1970, he did this in a rather dramatic way. He said (but in Latin):

> Almighty God, Father of our Lord Jesus Christ, who have given these your servants a new birth from water and the Holy Spirit, and have granted them remission of all sins, send into them from heaven your sevenfold Holy Spirit, the Counsellor. *Everyone replied: Amen!* The Spirit of **wisdom** and **understanding**. *Everyone replied: Amen!* The Spirit of **counsel** and **courage**. *Everyone replied: Amen!* The Spirit of **knowledge** and **reverence**. *Everyone replied: Amen!* Fill them with the Spirit of **awe** towards you; and in your mercy mark them out for eternal life by the sign of Christ's Cross. Through the same Jesus Christ, your Son, our Lord, who lives and reigns with you in the unity of the same Holy Spirit, as God, for ever and ever.
>
> *Everyone replied: Amen!*

Almost the same prayer is used today, but we only say one "Amen," at the end.

We call wisdom, understanding, counsel, courage, knowledge, reverence (or devotion) and awe (or "fear") "the Seven *Gifts* of the Holy Spirit." But, really, the Bishop calls down *the Spirit Himself.* As we start a new stage in our journey, God gives us a Friend to rely on. The Spirit is the Gift.

The Latin word *spiritus,* like the Greek *pneuma* and

the Hebrew *ruah*, can mean 'spirit', 'breath', 'wind', 'impulse'. God's Holy Spirit comes to impel, carry, inspire and guide us in these seven ways.

The gifts are given through Jesus

In this pamphlet, we shall see that the Holy Spirit, with His Gifts, is given us through Jesus. We shall explore why we need Him to guide us, and how He does so. First we shall do this in a general way; then we shall look at each of the Seven Gifts in turn.

'Confirmation' means 'Strengthening'. Before the core Rite of Confirmation, the Bishop invites us to ask the Father to pour out the Holy Spirit upon His adopted children, that the Spirit may strengthen them by the abundance of His gifts, and by His anointing bring them to perfection as conformed to Christ. Jesus is God's perfect and beloved Child, who was totally attuned to His Father's will. Through the Seven Gifts the Spirit makes us like Jesus and attunes us to the Father's ways.

All those who love God possess the Seven Gifts. After all, the Old Testament tells us of many people who were God's friends in the time before Christ came. They hoped for the Messiah God would send; they were conformed to Christ, some of them as Martyrs. They were led by the Spirit even though there was no

Confirmation. But the special commission given us in Confirmation makes the Spirit's guidance specially necessary. And so the Bishop who confirms us calls down upon us the Spirit who through wisdom, understanding, counsel, courage, knowledge, reverence and awe renders us sensitive to His own guidance.

Jesus hands on the Spirit to us

The prophet Isaiah saw that the Royal House of David, the son of Jesse, had become like a dried-up root, the stump of a cut-down tree. In chapter 11 of his book he predicted new life would spring from it – a new Messiah, a new anointed King:

> Now a Branch shall come forth from the stock of Jesse, and a Shoot shall blossom from his root. And the Spirit of the Lord shall abide upon him: the Spirit of **wisdom** and **understanding**, the Spirit of **counsel** and **strength**, the Spirit of **knowledge** and of **reverence** towards the Lord; and he shall savour **reverence** towards the Lord.

In this passage, the word 'reverence' appears twice. When the Old Testament was translated into Greek for Jews outside Palestine, the same word was rendered in two ways. When St Jerome translated the Bible into Latin, he drew on the original Hebrew, and on the Greek, to give us:

> ... the Spirit of the Lord shall abide upon him: the Spirit of **wisdom** and **understanding**, the Spirit of **counsel** and **courage**, the Spirit of **knowledge** and **reverence;** and the Spirit of **awe** towards the Lord shall fill him.

The Seven Spirits

This list of 'Seven Spirits' became part of the Rite of Confirmation. Teachers like Gregory the Great, Thomas Aquinas, and Bonaventure, reflected on the place of these Gifts in the Christian pilgrimage.

Jesus is the Messiah, the promised Son of David. He possesses the Gifts in their fullness. Immediately after His Baptism, the Holy Spirit appeared, and John the Baptist understood what this meant:

> I saw the Spirit coming down out of heaven like a dove, and He abode upon Him... the One who sent me to baptize with water said to me, "When you see the Spirit coming down and abiding on someone, He is it who will baptise with the Holy Spirit." (*Jn* 1:33)

Jesus had been conceived by the power of the Holy Spirit, as the One who would hand on the Spirit. But it was after His Baptism that Jesus was led by the Spirit to face down temptation and to begin His public ministry (*Mk* 1:12; *Lk* 4:1, 14, 18-21; *Ac* 10:38).

The autumn before He was crucified, Jesus promised to give the Holy Spirit to His followers:

"If any one thirst, let him come to me;
"And let him drink, whoever believes in me.
"As Scripture says: Rivers of living water shall flow out of his midst."

[The Evangelist adds:] He said this about the Spirit, whom those who came to faith in Him were to receive. For the Spirit wasn't yet on the scene, since Jesus had not yet been glorified. (*Jn* 7:37-39)

When Jesus was glorified – raised up on the Cross – He was like the rock that Moses struck to provide water (*Ex* 17:6), the new Temple from which Ezekiel saw health-giving water flow (*Ezk* 47:1), the pierced one Zechariah prophesied in connection with a cleansing fountain (*Zc* 12:10, 13:1). He bowed His head, and "handed over the Spirit" (*Jn* 19:30, translated literally). His side was pierced, and blood-and-water, *living* water, flowed (*Jn* 19:34-37).

The Holy Spirit came to us because of Jesus' Sacrifice, and keeps on coming. In each Sacrament, the power of Jesus' Sacrifice brings us the Holy Spirit – for a special purpose.

Risen from the dead, Jesus could say to His disciples what He still says to us at Confirmation: "Peace to you. Just as the Father has sent me, I in turn send you... Receive the Holy Spirit" (*Jn* 20:21-22). Having ascended into the

Father's glory, Jesus could pour out the Spirit with special power at the first Pentecost, so as to launch the Church (*Ac* 2:33). That power comes to us at Confirmation.

In the Old Testament, Kings and High Priests were anointed with perfumed oil. When David was anointed as King, the Spirit came upon him (1 *S* 16:13). So the term 'anointing' could be used for when the Spirit came, even if no oil was poured. Elijah anointed Elisha as Prophet by giving him a special share in the Spirit (1 *K* 19:16; 2 *K* 2:9). One of Isaiah's successors knew himself anointed by the Spirit to bring good news (*Is* 61:1). Jesus could claim that the text applied to Him (*Lk* 4:14-21) for He was anointed in the sense that He possessed the Spirit in an unlimited way, and had authority to hand on the Spirit. The same Anointing comes to us and teaches us (1 *Jn* 2:20, 27), and this is brought about dramatically by the use of Chrism in Confirmation.

In Confirmation we share Jesus' Anointing so as to share His public ministry. The Spirit who led Jesus to make God's mercy and loyalty audible, visible and tangible, leads us to do the same. The Spirit who empowered Jesus to face down temptation, empowers us to do the same.

The Holy Spirit's guidance in the Bible

In ancient times, most nations worshipped many 'gods'; these personified the capricious and conflicting forces of nature, or were seen as the spirits that kept the heavens moving inexorably.

The Old Testament says: "Hear, O Israel, the Lord our God, the Lord is One" (*Dt* 6:4). There is only one real God. In Him there are no conflicting forces: He is One. He is not capricious or aloof; He is *our* God, He has shown us His loyalty.

God revealed His Name Lord to Moses (*Ex* 3:13-15). When the Jews meet the Name in the Bible they say *Adonai* ("my Lord"); Christians inherited that custom. The ancient Hebrew word *yhwh* can mean "He is causing things to be" and "His Being is resplendent." God possesses being in its fullness; every thing exists only because He loves it into being.

So God is mysterious and incomprehensible – but also deeply close to us as He holds us in being.

The Old Testament speaks of God's "Word" and "Wisdom" as creating the world's beauty and forming God's people. Word and Wisdom are not like angels that God creates and sends. They are *God,* truly with us. But by expressing God's presence in such ways, the Old Testament reminds us of His awesome majesty.

The Creator Spirit

Likewise the Spirit is not a creature. In the poetry of *Is* 40:13, "Who has directed the Spirit of the Lord?" and

"Who as His counsellor has instructed the Lord?" are two ways of saying the same thing. The Spirit is Creator: "By the Word of the Lord the heavens were made, and all their host by the *Breath* of His mouth" (*Ps* 33:6 – the same word, *ruah*, means breath, wind, spirit).

Evil spirits can "take people over". The Holy Spirit might be "impulsive" – see for example 1 *S* 10:10 – but is typically empowering, enabling, life-enhancing. After all, He is the Creator who makes us be; He is not in competition with us, unless we choose to be in conflict with Him and "grieve the Holy Spirit" (*Is* 63:10). So the Spirit works within and alongside God's friends. He gives life (e.g. in *Ps* 104:29-30); prophecy (*Ezk* 11:5; *Mi* 3:8); leadership (1 *S* 16:13); skill (*Ex* 31:3); holiness (*Ezk* 36:27); wisdom (*Jb* 32:8; *Ws* 9:17); guidance (*Ps* 143:10).

The Trinity

Jesus is Lord (*Jn* 20:28; 1 *Co* 12:3). His Name means "YHWH saves" (cf. *Mt* 1:21-23). His exaltation proves the Name above all others – YHWH – is His (*Ph* 2:9). He is equal to God the Father (*Jn* 5:18).

This does not mean that God is, after all, not One (*Mk* 12:29). Jesus is *One with* the Father (*Jn* 10:30). There is a "Father-Son relationship" "within" the One God – a relationship we are invited into! Jesus gives us "power to become children of God" (Jn 1:12)!

Jesus is the Word in whom the Father expresses Himself fully (*Jn* 1:1, 14:9), the Wisdom who is God the Father's perfect Image (compare *Jn* 1:9, *Col* 1:15 and *Heb* 1:2-3 with *Ws* 7:24-27). He has come as man to make the Father known (*Jn* 1:14, 18).

The infinite mystery and majesty which belong fully to the Father, belong fully to Jesus as God – and fully to another: the Holy Spirit. At the Last Supper, Jesus spoke of how the Spirit would come as "another Counsellor" because of His (Jesus') "going away", that is, His Passion, Death and Resurrection (*Jn* 14:16, 26, 16:7).

"Counsellor" translates *Parakletos,* which means "Advocate" (counsel for the defence) and "one who gives counsel and encouragement". The Spirit is the Friend to stand by us to advise us and to provide us with the right words when our Faith and Hope are challenged (*Mt* 10:19-20). The Father is our Friend, the Son is our Friend (*Jn* 15:15), the Spirit is our Friend – each in His distinctive way.

The Spirit is Lord (2 *Co* 3:17); He is One God with the Father and the Son – They have one Name (*Mt* 28:19).

A New Creation

In the New Testament, the Spirit does what He does in the Old Testament: He gives life (2 *Co* 3:6); prophecy (*Lk* 1:41-42; *Ac* 19:6, 21:11; *Ep* 3:5); leadership (*Ac*

20:28; 2 *Tm* 1:6-7); skill (1 *Co* 12:4-11); holiness (1 *Co* 6:11; 1 *P* 1:2); wisdom (1 *Co* 2:4-16); guidance (*Ac* 8:29, 16:6-7). There is a danger of grieving Him (*Ep* 4:30).

Having been active in the original creation, the Spirit brings about a *new* creation, and His presence in us is the down-payment on what He will complete on the Last Day (*Rm* 8:9-11, 23; 2 *Co* 1:22, 5:5; *Ep* 1:13-14).

We glimpse how the Spirit is the Bond of Love and Joy between and enfolding Father and Son. The Spirit hovers between Them at Jesus' Baptism (*Mk* 1:10). Jesus rejoiced in the Holy Spirit when He gave thanks to the Father (*Lk* 10:21). It was in the Spirit that Jesus offered Himself to the Father (*Heb* 9:14). So, the same Spirit hovers over us when we are baptized, to join us to the Father as His beloved children. When we celebrate the Eucharist, we are enfolded in the Spirit's unity so that we can give thanks, honour and glory to the Father in, through and with the Son.

So the Counsellor is the Anointing and the Living Water. His presence was revealed by tongues of fire (*Ac* 2:2). Fire is difficult to see in itself, but things placed in it will glow. The Spirit makes us radiant with words of truth and deeds of love. Water enters living things to make them thrive. When one is anointed with oil, the oil is not seen, but the skin becomes radiant. Chrism, the tangible sign of the anointing Spirit's coming, expresses the radiance the Spirit gives us. Its perfume, is a sign of how we must spread "the sweet fragrance of Christ" (2 *Co* 2:15).

Images of the Spirit

The words we translate as 'Spirit' can mean wind, and the Spirit is the Wind that blows where He will (*Jn* 3:8, cf. *Ac* 2:2). The wind is the air we breathe, it sustains us all the time; just now and then it gives us a push. So the Spirit sustains us, and we take Him for granted; now and then He surprises us.

All these images for the Spirit are 'intimate' and 'tactful'. The Spirit does not "put Himself forward" but forms us in the depths of our being into those who welcome Christ, the Word of God (*Catechism of the Catholic Church*, 687), and who, in and like Christ, will be transparent to God the Father, channels of His goodness (*Mt* 5:16, 48).

The other image of the Spirit is the dove (*Lk* 3:22), which of old had signalled the start of a new age of mercy and divine loyalty (*Gn* 8:8-9:17), a mercy and loyalty which took flesh in Jesus (*Jn* 1:17), and must take flesh in us, His Body, called in the Spirit to share His mission (*Jn* 20:21-22).

So as we reflect on how the seven-fold Spirit guides us, we will be open to those occasions when, like the wind, He “gives us a push” to help us on our way – or to change our path! But we will expect most of His guidance to be so intimate that it is hidden – hidden from us, but not so often hidden from those whom He inspires us to help. This is not because the Spirit is an impersonal force, but because He is the Friend whose company is like the air we breathe.

The Spirit in our lives

The resources the Spirit gives us for the journey

Because the human being is the most complex thing in the universe, we need lots of resources if we are to function well and reach fulfilment – and, in a fallen world, if our sinfulness is to be healed.

We are one Body in Christ. The Spirit gives different talents to different members, so that we can help each other journey into God. St Paul discusses these "charismatic gifts" in 1 Corinthians 12 – and warns us against priding ourselves on them. We may even need to hide a talent to give space to others (1 *Co* 14:26-33)! It is possible to have valuable gifts, yet lack Love (1 *Co* 13:1-2). In fact, many of these gifts are temporary (13:8). They are often needed for particular occasions, then become redundant. We can be prevented from exercising them by persecution, illness and retirement. For the present life, Faith, Hope and Love *abide* (1 *Co* 13:13) – from the beginning to the end of our Christian pilgrimage, we need *these* God-given resources.

Faith will be replaced by Sight (2 *Co* 5:7), Hope by Possession (*Rm* 8:24-25). Love is the highest of the Spirit's gifts (1 *Co* 12:31) for it never ends – in heaven, when we see God, it becomes all the stronger – and it alone ensures we use other gifts in humble service.

Virtue

We call Faith, Hope and Charity "Theological Virtues". A 'virtue' is a *strength* and *nobility* of mind or character. These three strengths are from God and join us to God. By Faith we undertake a journey in Christ to the God we cannot yet see (*Heb* 11:1-12:2). Hope founded on God's power and love (not on our own innate strength or merit) provides energy for so immense a journey. Charity is a God-given – a "God-shaped" – Love by which we embrace God our Goal. It is a Friendship with God whose happiness we hope to share. By it we share our Friend's concerns; we share God's own love for ourselves and all those He gives us to care for. We share God's thirst that we, our family and friends – even our enemies – will enjoy God's company for ever.

Strength

We need many other strengths of mind and character. Some are developed by our parents and teachers, then by our own practice, building on innate resources and correcting innate disorders. When he shapes us in Love, the Holy Spirit brings lots of other strengths of mind and will, to heal our weakness and to make us able to run the course set before us. Charity sets the goal for all these virtues, since it makes God our 'top priority'.

We also have laws to guide us: the Natural Law written on our hearts (*Rm* 2:15); the Moral Precepts given in the Old Testament that remind us of the Natural Law; the rules laid down there for the life of the People of Israel as a model for future statesmen and stateswomen as they make wise laws for new circumstances; the New Law given by Jesus, for example in the Sermon on the Mount (*Mt* 5-7). We need not be "*under* Law" (*Ga* 5:18), for the Holy Spirit sets us free (2 *Co* 3:17) by leading us by love to do with joy what the Laws require, and more besides (*Ga* 5:13-6:2).

All these God-given resources – Law from without, Virtues from within – are still not enough! For St Thomas Aquinas, the Seven Gifts of the Holy Spirit are something else again: they enable us to sense the Spirit guiding us to do more than the Law requires. They add elements of divine spontaneity and divine instinct that allow our life in Christ to be vibrant.

The Holy Spirit as the friend to guide us when our resources are inadequate

When St Thomas explores why we need the Seven Gifts (*Summa Theologiae, Prima Secundae* 68), he explains that they are not 'charismatic gifts' in the sense of talents that *some* people have so that they can help others. Nor are they virtues, 'God-given *strengths'*, like Faith, Hope and Charity. Isaiah speaks of them as "spirits" – the spirit of wisdom, the spirit of counsel, the spirit of coThey are to do with impulse, drive, guidance, *inspiration*. They are to do with the Holy Spirit Himself prompting us, leading us, taking us by the hand, giving us the instinct to do what must be done, in the divine way it must be done.

Sharing in the life of God

True, the Seven Gifts are real 'qualities' in us. This does not mean they are "further resources" that we can deploy. It means that *we are really attuned* to the Holy Spirit as *He* deploys us as members of Christ, sharing His mission and journeying together into His glory.

If our project were simply to live a good *human* life, we would be able to work out what needs doing, we would be able to 'take charge' of our lives. In a fallen world this is not easy. The virtues, the good patterns of thinking and desiring that enable us to live well, are built up with help and effort. But, in principle, human reason can work out how we should live so that we flourish – especially if citizens work together, law-givers have good moral sense, and leaders are concerned for the common good.

We have a *divine* project! We are called *to share the divine nature* (2 *P* 1:4), to be on our way to the inheritance due to us as God's children (*Rm* 8:17, 23). We cannot fathom the greatness of our Christian lives, for in Baptism we have died with Christ, and begun a new life in Him – and for the time being this life is "hidden with Christ in God" (*Col* 3:1-4, cf. 1 *Jn* 3:1-2). Only the tip of an iceberg is seen as it floats in the ocean; our Christian life is an 'upside-down iceberg' hanging down into this world from the 'ocean' that is God. By God's grace, our lives have a *supernatural* dimension – not a 'spooky' dimension, but a *God-like* dimension. And so we are "out of our depth".

Vocation

Faith gives us a glimpse of God's plan – but not all the details we should like to know. We don't yet see clearly how God is guiding creation so that "all things work together for the good" of His friends (*Rm* 8:28). Hope gives us the energy to press on – but does not teach us the precise steps to take.

Of course, the Natural Law, civic laws, the Church's laws and teachings, Scripture, the advice of others, common sense – and Jesus' example – give us much welcome direction. But they aren't tramlines determining our every move. Often we cannot see how some big or small decision will help or hinder our growth into God, or other people's growth into God. Usually it is clear what a human being and a child of God must *not* do. Often it is not clear precisely what this child of God *should* do in this particular situation. Yet doing the right thing can be very important.

I had to decide whether to join a religious order, or remain a scientist and get married. Both would have been possible, both fulfilling and enjoyable, challenging and demanding. There was no law to tell me which was my duty. I could not *know* which course would be better for me, for both ways of life involve temptations and dangers. I could not *know* in which way I might touch more people's lives for good. "Thinking things through" was not enough: I had to pray for guidance, look for hints from God, and trust that the instinct that came was indeed from God.

Inspiration

If you are about to visit a lonely relative, and a friend phones who is in some distress, do you put off the visit, and talk to your friend? You cannot help but let someone down, whichever course you take. And what do you say to your friend, if you do talk to her? How can you know that your words will bring strength and comfort? You have no chance to plan them. A quick prayer to the Holy Spirit entrusts to Him the decision you make, and invites Him to guide the flow of the conversation.

Not all our moral problems are to do with our sinfulness, or other people's sinfulness. Some puzzles arise because we don't have a "God's eye view" of the whole sweep of our personal histories.

Obviously, even citizens of Earth can be faced with awkward decisions, where the best way forward is not clear. If we are citizens of Heaven (*Heb* 11:13-16; 12:22, 28; 13:14) "the stakes are higher", the good to be achieved – or obstructed – is greater. Hence we need *the guidance of the Holy Spirit.* Through Charity He shapes our desires and our *priorities* to ensure we love God most. This naturally influences our thinking. But in all sorts of detailed ways, we need the Holy Spirit to give us the right thoughts, the right instincts, the right decisions, so that God's love takes flesh in the fabric of our lives.

Spending life in the right ministry, or with the right spouse, can make the journey into God that much more smooth and secure for countless people. Speaking the right word to someone can make us a channel of God's love and truth. Through us, God is helping that person go forward on pilgrimage. When we abide together in God, we will rejoice together over the ways we have helped each other reach Him. For the moment, *we are not able to master the journey.* We cannot be in totally confident control of how things are working out under

God's Providence; the Spirit must prompt and inspire us so that our journey – and other people's journeys – sweetly and surely reach their Goal.

We cannot possess or "own" our lives; they belong to God, and are *His* "craftsmanship" (*Ep* 2:10). We cannot pretend to be fully in control of every outcome, nor even of every step we take. We must place our hands in the Holy Spirit's hand, in words such as Cardinal Newman's:

> Lead, kindly Light, amid th'encircling gloom,
>   Lead Thou me on;
> The night is dark, and I am far from home:
>   Lead Thou me on.
> Keep Thou my feet; I do not ask to see
> The distant scene; one step enough for me.

When we look at the individual Gifts of the Holy Spirit, we will see that they do for us what they did for Jesus! He had to press forward on the Way God the Father had marked out for Him – and it was a Way that people did not expect the Messiah should follow. Jesus did not have to fight against vices within Himself, unlike us. But He did have to fight against false advice as well as natural fears. When several possibilities were open to Him, He had to choose the right one by a divine instinct. He did all this in the strength of the Holy Spirit – and so must we.

Being attuned to the Holy Spirit

We have seen how deeply we depend on the Holy Spirit to draw and move our hearts and minds. This does *not* mean we are puppets in the hand of God. Quite the opposite! It does not mean we sit back and do nothing, not bothering to study our Faith, not needing to think seriously about moral issues. Quite the opposite.

The 'gods' of the old pagan myths were limited; they competed for influence with each other, and with us. Like the evil spirits we hear of in the Bible, they could 'take people over' so that their personalities disappeared. The Oracle at Delphi went into something like a drug-induced trance so that Apollo could speak through her. Where there was more of the 'god', there was less of woman or man.

Father, Son and Spirit are YHWH: "He is making things to be." They do not compete for influence; they do not take people over so that their personalities disappear. YHWH makes us to be what and who we are, and delights in the perfecting of what He is making. Where there is more of the true God's work, there is *more* of woman and of man. This is especially the case when the true God abides within us (*Jn* 14:15-23). The Holy Spirit abides within us to form us into the Father's beloved children, to 'shape' us into Christ's likeness, and to be our Paraclete, our Friend for the Campaign.

For example, the Holy Spirit is the true Author of the Bible. It says exactly what He willed it to say. But if you read the Bible in the original Hebrew and Greek, you hear the human authors and editors putting *themselves* at the service of God and of us. Their personalities, hopes and fears are all there. The Spirit was at work in and through St Paul's impetuous way of dictating, St John's affectionate pondering of Jesus' personality, St Luke's skill at imitating different styles of writing.

Shakespeare, Mozart, Einstein, and so on, had outstanding gifts. These are from the Creator Spirit – *and* they are part of the personalities of these people. The same Spirit does remarkable things through great Saints and Leaders in the Church – Catherine of Siena, Francis Xavier, Mother Theresa, John Paul II... But when we read their lives or their writings, *we meet these people,* not automatons.

So, when the Holy Spirit leads any of God's children to do what should be done, "let them give thanks to him by whom they act. For *they are acted upon so that they may act,* not in the sense that they do nothing themselves" (St Augustine, *On Correction and Grace* II, 4). By the Holy Spirit's action within us, *we ourselves* act well and lovingly.

A bond of love not possession

Unlike evil spirits, the Holy Spirit does not 'possess' us – except in the way expressed in the Song of Songs 2:16:

"My beloved is mine and I am his". He has made us *His friends*; in friendship He gives Himself, so that *we* possess *Him*! He brings us integrity, self-possession, the ability to put ourselves wholeheartedly into what is really good for us. Sin is slavery (*Jn* 8:34), it makes us labour for what is not satisfying (*Is* 55:2). The Spirit grants freedom (2 *Co* 3:17). He makes us aware of Who is really good for us, and liberates us to journey into Him.

The Spirit creates in us all the resources we spoke of above: special talents, the strengths of mind and character that are called virtues, God-like resources of belief and trust, a determined love for God. He sustains our persevering use of these qualities day by day. But the Spirit also creates *new* things in us, maybe many times each day, each hour. New insights into the beauty of God's ways. New words to say when new conversations must begin. New thoughts of good things to be done. New feelings of wonder and awe at God's greatness and at His plans for the people around us. A sense of what should be done when a new decision or difficulty confronts us. Without this constant creativity on the part of the Spirit, we cannot go forward into God, we would stagnate. And so we depend on the Living Water continually welling up in us (*Jn* 4:14) to lead us to eternal life. We need the prompting, inspiration, creative energy of the Spirit always going beyond, taking us beyond, what is already in us.

The 'Seven Spirits', seven 'inputs', of wisdom and understanding, counsel and courage, knowledge, reverence and awe, represent the ways in which the initiative must always lie with the Holy Spirit, not with us. He must be beside and within us, not just to sustain the resources He has given, but also to give us the input they cannot provide. He must point out the next step for us to take, He must keep the journey going. The Spirit is the Divine Wind that fills our sails making the voyage that He draws us to undertake more exhilarating, and ensuring its success. This is specially necessary since the Goal of this voyage is 'over the horizon'.

The boat must turn its sails into the Divine Wind, so as to run home before It. So, the Seven Gifts are *gifts*, are something the Spirit has created within us, are real qualities of ours. Not extra resources, but forms of receptivity. They are the ways we are rendered sensitive to the Spirit's initiatives, attuned to the Spirit's teaching, enabled to listen to the Spirit's advice, 'moveable' by that Divine Impulse.

On the wavelength of the Spirit

The Seven Gifts of the Holy Spirit ensure that we are "on the Spirit's wavelength". As a friendship deepens, and especially in a loving marriage, each comes to sense what the other is thinking, they grow in sensitivity to each other, in sym-pathy ('feeling together'). Colleagues who work closely together are attuned to each other's trains of thought. A good tutor knows what will help her student learn best – and the student becomes increasingly open to her tutor's message. A 'master-craftsman' and his apprentice become a single team. If, by Charity, the Holy Spirit is our Friend, we are in an 'enabling relationship' with Him: He does not 'dominate' us, but helps us become and be and find our*selves.* He evokes a sensitivity to Himself; we receive Him as our Teacher and 'master-craftsman'. We naturally, instinctively, become open to His message, able to work with Him as He works in and with us.

Naturally, we should pray to the Holy Spirit to "tune us more and more to His wavelength", for example in the words of Edwin Hatch's hymn:

Breathe on me, Breath of God,
Fill me with life anew,
That I may love what Thou dost love,
And do what Thou wouldst do.

Breathe on me, Breath of God,
Until my heart is pure,
Until with Thee I will one will
To do and to endure.

Growing in love

As Love grows, so does our instinctive feel for the Spirit's ways. In the earlier stages of their journeys, many great Saints were almost buffeted by the Spirit blowing where He would. His guidance became more quiet, more unobtrusive as they 'developed a taste' for His direction, as their minds and wills and hearts became more open to God.

Even if Charity has not begun to burn very intensely in us, we can expect the Spirit to move us sweetly and gently – if also powerfully – in ways we aren't always aware of. After all, He often opens our eyes and ears to see and hear Jesus, Jesus in His Sacraments, Jesus in the Scriptures, Jesus in His Church, Jesus in those who need our love or, better, His love through us. The Spirit does not often encourage us to waste time looking into ourselves. When He does, it's often to see how far we have to grow.

Testing the Spirits

If we keep opening ourselves to the Holy Spirit in prayer (that's the one prayer the Father is *always* willing to grant – see *Lk* 11:13), if we seek to grow in God's friendship, we can trust the Spirit to be at work in the 'heights and depths' of our thinking, enlightening and directing us quietly. All the same, not every idea that pops into our heads is from the Holy Spirit! All sorts of silly ideas occur to people; we often mentally try out possibilities that we come to realise are not worth pursuing. In his First Letter (4:1-3) St John tells us to 'test the spirits':

> Beloved, do not believe every inspiration, but test inspirations to see if they are from God. For many false prophets have gone abroad into the world. This is how you are to know God's Inspiration: every inspiration that acknowledges that Jesus Christ has come in the flesh is from God. But every inspiration that does not acknowledge Jesus is not from God. [I have translated *pneuma*, spirit, as 'inspiration', to try to get John's point across.]

If some purported insight does not fit with the basic Christian message, we can discount it. If it helps us understand better the real Jesus and what he taught us, we can take it seriously. The same is true of courses of action that occur to us. Do they fit with the natural law that the Old Testament reminds us of and Jesus affirms? Do they build up the Church? Do they stand to make us better disciples of Jesus? If the answer to such questions is 'Yes', we can take them seriously. If 'No', we can put them down to our own roving imagination, to peer pressure, even, sometimes, to Satan's suggestions.

Growing in faith and knowledge

So we are not meant to abandon our *efforts* to grow in knowledge and virtue, relying on every whim that comes as if we could presume on God to 'save us without us'. We are committed by our Baptism and Confirmation to study our Faith, to cherish the Scriptures, to receive the Sacraments devoutly, to read the Church's teaching and the great Doctors of the Church, to practise our Faith and our Love, to get used to doing good and unfamiliar with doing evil. When we are confronted by moral issues, we must think them through carefully, taking advice from wise people, and especially from the Church's Tradition. That is what it means to 'form our conscience' – for conscience is not a 'gut reaction' (we should not trust those), it is a carefully-thought-through decision about what we should do or what we have done. All this work is of course granted us by the Holy Spirit, who forms Christ and Christ's mind within us, so that we may 'grow up into Christ'. This results in a broader and deeper sensitivity to God's plan, and ensures that we do not resist the Holy Spirit and play false to His friendship (*Ep* 3:14-4:30).

So study, learning, law, Church policy, discussion, and careful thought on the one hand, and the Spirit's voice on the other, are not in tension with each other. One and the same Spirit speaks in the Scriptures, preserves the mind of Christ in the Church, grants leadership, guides Popes, Bishops and Councils – and whispers in the depths of our heart. All the public, humdrum and laborious work the Spirit empowers, makes us more able to distinguish His voice when He speaks through all the clamour of false ideas that assail us from within and without. In and through the whole fabric of Christian living, the Spirit 'hones' our sym-pathy with Him, makes us more ready to learn His lessons, to think His thoughts, to hold His hand, to go with Him on those occasions when we need His inspiration.

In the Sacraments, and in all the exercise of practical Charity, the Spirit builds up the Seven Gifts within us, to give us 'a feel for His ways', a 'taste' for His manoeuvres, an instinct for what He is telling us, an ability to tune in to His voice and ignore what contradicts His policy. In Confirmation, above all, He commits Himself to do this for us, and commits us to follow Jesus who, in the Spirit, was obedient unto death and remained in perfect communion with His Father.

The Seven Gifts

Awe towards the God who deserves our all

The last of the Seven Gifts called down on us at Confirmation is "the Fear of the Lord". We begin our discussion of the individual Gifts by looking at Fear, because Psalm 111:10 tells us: "The Fear of the Lord is the beginning of Wisdom". Fear is the most basic element in being on God's wavelength, Wisdom the highest.

Of course, we can be afraid of several things. We are naturally afraid of poverty and pain, humiliation and loneliness, sickness and death. Sometimes such fears can hold us back from doing what we should, and must be countered by the virtue – even the Gift – of Courage.

We can be afraid of separation from God. If we are in a state of serious sin, if we are rebelling against God and resisting His love, then we have cut ourselves off from God. But the Holy Spirit has not cast us off. He can lead us to be afraid of the consequences of our sins. A fear of spending eternity without the God who alone can fulfil us can prompt us to repent. This kind of fear is not one of the Seven Gifts, since it comes to us before we are restored to God's friendship. St Thomas calls it 'servile fear' – the kind of fear felt by a slave who finds his master's commands unwelcome. St John speaks of this kind of fear when he says: "There is no fear in love, but perfect love casts out fear. For fear has to do with punishment, and he who fears is not perfected in love" (1 *Jn* 4:18). If God were to leave us alone to choose eternity without Him, this would be a punishment!

In Confession, the Sacrament of Repentance, the Holy Spirit changes our hearts and minds. Once again, we make God our 'top priority' and want to walk in His ways. We are restored to Love, and are 'on the Spirit's wavelength'. As God's beloved children, we need have no fear of separation from Him. His Love for us is a Covenant, a pledge of loyalty; He will keep us secure in His love and give us strength to remain loyal to Him.

There is a kind of fear which does go with love. Husband and wife should not be afraid of each other, but – because they love each other – they should be afraid of letting each other down. Maybe the husband likes watching cricket, but sees that it's important for him to accompany his wife to visit her lonely aunt some week-end. So he goes with his wife, and gives up watching an important cricket match.

St Thomas calls this kind of sensitivity 'filial fear' – it's the concern a loving child would have not to offend a parent. It is a Gift of the Holy Spirit, for it is a deep concern to do what pleases God and avoid what we recognise would hinder our journey into Him. It leads us to imitate Jesus' self-sacrifice.

One time, Jesus and His disciples were too busy even to eat (*Mk* 6:30-34). Prudently, Jesus told them to come away and rest. When they got to a lonely place, they found lots of people had already got there, needing to be taught. So Jesus did not rest, but taught them. He gave up His human, physical needs – that was a *divine* act of self-sacrifice. We sometimes need to sacrifice even quite sensible needs, and change carefully-made plans, if we are to be channels of God's care to others, and grow towards Him. It is difficult to know when and how to give up good things; sometimes we have an *important duty* to care for ourselves. We need a kind of divine instinct if we are to perform the *right* divine deeds of self-sacrifice; the Holy Spirit gives us that instinct as and when we need it. Sensitivity to His prompting in this area is provided by the Gift of Fear. After all, not every thought of self-sacrifice is an impulse from God; it may be a romantic dream, or an escapism that doesn't engage with the real demands God makes on us!

Our love for pleasure, comfort and security is not perfectly balanced, and we can let it draw us away from God. Our trust in God is mixed with a fear of letting

Him down. So our share in Jesus' self-sacrifice includes a personal fight against sinfulness; the Spirit leads us to "put to death what is earthly in us" (*Col* 3:5). Jesus' supreme knowledge and love of His Father meant that in Him there was no sinfulness, no fear of separation from God. When we enjoy the Vision of God in Heaven we too will be beyond any such fear.

But Jesus did have the Gift of Fear, St Thomas points out, and so will we even when we are in Heaven! In the English version of the Rite of Confirmation, 'fear of you' is translated as 'Wonder and Awe in your presence'. This Wonder and Awe comes from knowing that God is YHWH, the One who alone possesses being and alone can grant it. If we really experienced how profound is our dependence on God for our very being, we would be overwhelmed with His greatness, and sense how deserving He is of our obedience. We would appreciate more deeply the privilege of ministering His care to those He wants us to nurture, by breaking our sleep to look after our babies or patients or parishioners, or by other forms of sacrifice. The Holy Spirit led St Catherine of Siena to say to God, "You are He Who Is; I am she who is not," and eagerly spend her life in service of God's People.

A dancer sometimes holds his partner's hands and whirls round so that her feet leave the floor. If he were to let go, she might end up in the orchestra pit! But she trusts him to hold on. When the Spirit lets us glimpse – with a kind of vertigo – how God holds us in being, He also enkindles our trust that God will not let us fall into nothingness. Jesus knew that He drew life from the Father (*Jn* 6:57), and we begin to share now that overwhelming sense of dependence that goes with thanksgiving and love, and shall be both greater and more confident in Heaven.

Courage

Fear of offending the Lord can arm us against letting desire for pleasure lead us into sin. It can prompt us to sacrifice our needs so as to minister God's care to others. But speaking of being armed leads us on to another Gift. For threats and dangers can also put us off our journey into God.

In some societies it is dangerous to become a Christian – it can lose you your job, your freedom, your family, your life. In our own society a nurse or doctor who stands by Catholic moral principles (which in medical matters are simply basic human moral principles) might lose her job or the chance of promotion. We might be ridiculed for following what we recognise as our vocation, or admitting that we say our prayers.

Pagan and Christian moral thinkers have recognised *courage* as a key *virtue*. It strengthens us to face dangers, making us neither cowardly nor foolhardy. This virtue is not enough if we are to share Jesus' own divine victory. We need the Gift of the Holy Spirit that is called Courage.

Sometimes the dangers we face are so terrible that we need the Holy Spirit to stand by us lest we give way. The greatest act of Courage is Martyrdom. Many Saints have braved torture and death for God's sake. The Holy Spirit accompanied them as He accompanied Jesus. Jesus plucked up courage to go to Jerusalem the autumn before He died (*Jn* 7:8-14), to go back to that area and raise Lazarus, which would prove the last straw (*Jn* 11:1-9, 45-53), to accept His approaching Death (*Jn* 12:23-28). In the Garden He put aside His natural fear of death and prayed that He might accomplish His Father's will (*Mt* 26:36-46). Crucifixion was so cruel, and so much depended on Jesus going through with it, that all this was no mere human 'plucking up courage' – it was *in the eternal Spirit* that Jesus offered Himself (*Heb* 9:14). In that Divine Love, He identified Himself to the soldiers so as to save His friends from death (*Jn* 18:4-9).

Moral virtues are deployed by *Prudence*, which is not excessive caution, but a strength of mind, the ability to think clearly in moral matters and make sound judgments. Some acts of Courage can *seem* so imprudent that we need a sound *instinct* from the Holy Spirit if we are to remain true. St John Fisher held out against the other Bishops of England as well as against the King; St Athanasius held out against nearly all the Bishops of the East.

We have met truly courageous people who have given up a career so as to care for a sick parent or spouse, or to become a missionary. Women abandoned by their husbands, who have not remarried, and have brought up children without the support of a new 'husband', because they knew their original marriage remained valid. People whose children have got into trouble, or become mentally ill, and have refused to stop trying to help, braving all rejection. All around us, the Holy Spirit is making His friends bold enough to soldier on, against what 'worldly' advice would say.

When she was very young, St Teresa of Avila set off to be martyred by the Moors – she hadn't got far before her parents caught her! Instead of that immature fantasy, the Spirit gave her courage for the real, more demanding task she was called to undertake. The Spirit who emboldens some people to die for God, emboldens many people to live for God. It takes courage to persevere with marriage, with parenthood, with friendships, with the demands of our jobs – to see the ever-fresh opportunities for reflecting God's joy into the humdrum and repetitive. It takes courage to persevere with life when we seem to meet one setback after another. It takes courage to keep on going to Confession and saying sorry for our sins, when Satan wants our moral difficulties to lead us into despair.

The *virtue* of Courage helps us *come through* dangers and complete demanding projects. We need the Gift of Courage, St Thomas suggests, because we have to submit to dying with Christ. We may have to leave projects unfinished for the sake of Martyrdom, or a vocation, or the need to care for someone. We cannot 'own' those we have nurtured, but must often allow them to grow up and follow their own vocation, while we entrust them to God's Providence. Through the Gift of Courage, the Holy Spirit who often leads us to keep going, can enable us to let go and yield ourselves into the Father's hands. With Julian of Norwich, we admit that we cannot yet see how "all manner thing shall be well". At the Last Judgment we will see how life and death, success and frustration, commitment and sacrifice, have all been part of our share in Jesus' passing over through death to new life. For the moment, we pray boldly, asking to be brave in our Faith, secure in our Hope.

Reverence for God our Father and for those he gives us to care for

We need the Spirit of the Seven Gifts to guide us because of the uncertainties of our present journey. We need the

Seven Gifts of the Spirit so as to be attuned to the Spirit who guides us, so as to be conformed to Christ, and so as to share the perspective of God the Father.

One of our present uncertainties is how to behave towards others. Clearly we need to minister God's own love to them (which is no mean task!) What is not always certain is exactly *how* to do this. When someone is in distress, what words of comfort do I speak? If someone I know is behaving badly, I may be called to exercise 'fraternal correction'. A tendency to over-react may tempt me to speak harshly. I may want to score a point. Instead, I should speak words that build up, chosen to help the other person grow. I may be tempted to hold back from speaking because of a fear of being rebuffed – to stand by and watch my friend suffer. Instead, should I take the risk of friendship? But what if almost anything I could say would build up resentment, would make things worse?

We need an instinct for 'getting it right', a 'feel' for the right approach. We need the Holy Spirit's guidance. By the Gift of Reverence the Spirit prompts us to say and do the right thing, at the right time, in the right way. His prompting *may* be 'counter-intuitive' – Jesus spoke with unexpected gentleness to sinners, and with unexpected sharpness to the pious, so as to help both grow.

Reverence, or Devotion, translates the Latin *pietas*.

That originally meant the respect children must have for their parents, and therefore came to mean devotion to God our Father. But St Gregory the Great turned it round: the Piety which is a Gift of the Spirit is the heartfelt mercy that leads us to help others. By this Gift, we *share God's own reverence*, God's own devotion, God's own cherishing, towards all His children. We share His vision for them. We become channels of God's own 'tactful mercy' towards those He nurtures.

At the same time, Reverence does enable us to share Jesus' Piety towards God the Father, as well as His approach to others. Jesus was devoted to His Father (*Jn* 8:29, etc.), and expressed this in prayer and thanksgiving towards the One He called "Abba!". We are privileged to share His devotion, His prayer, His thanksgiving. The Spirit leads us to cry out, "Abba, Father!" (*Rm* 8:15-16). We do this above all in the Holy Eucharist. By the Consecration of bread and wine to become Christ's Body and Blood, Christ's Sacrifice is made present, so we enjoy the result of the Sacrifice, the coming of the Holy Spirit – each Mass is a new Pentecost. Enfolded by the Holy Spirit, we can say, 'Our Father'.

We share Jesus' prayer, but we don't always know what to pray for while we hope for what we do not yet see. So the Spirit prompts us to pray, and if our prayer involves entrusting someone or some outcome to God's care, then in the depths of that prayer He expresses a longing for the God who will satisfy our needs beyond our imagining (*Rm* 8:25-27).

Listening to the Spirit's Advice

Part of being morally good involves not doing what law forbids. Some things are always wrong and must never be done, such as directly killing the innocent. But quite a few *detailed* laws aren't meant to cover every possible eventuality, and such laws can be set aside in exceptional circumstances. For example, the Church can dispense from procedures she has laid down; an ambulance driver can break the speed limit if it is clearly safe to do so and observing it would endanger, not preserve, life. The virtue of *equity* helps us promote the good at which a law is aiming, when wooden application of the law would hinder its purpose.

Often, when a law commands us to do something, we still have to work out when and how to do it. Very often, in big and small issues, there is no law to tell us what to do or avoid. Being morally good is a bigger thing than 'keeping the law'. We have to exercise the virtue of *Prudence.* This involves *asking advice* and *thinking carefully* – though we also need to be ready for snap decisions when there is little time to discuss the issue, or even think.

Asking advice and thinking carefully can be called 'taking counsel'. Since we are caught up in a divine project, and since we don't have a 'God's-eye-view' of all eventualities and connections, "the reckonings of mortals are faint-hearted, and their resolutions precarious" (*Ws* 9:14). Hence we must turn to the Holy Spirit, the Counsellor, asking *Him* for His advice, asking *Him* to direct our thinking. The Gift of Counsel helps us welcome His advice; shaped by it, our thoughts can be steered by Him to reach *right judgments* that He will embolden us to put into effect.

Before focusing on preaching rather than on healing, Jesus prayed (*Mk* 1:35). Before choosing the Twelve, He prayed (*Lk* 6:12). Before choosing Judas' replacement, the disciples prayed (*Ac* 1:24).

If we ask the Father to send us the Counsellor, if we entrust ourselves to His direction, should we expect to 'hear voices' telling us what to do? Usually, 'hearing voices' is a sign of psychological disturbance! We saw above that the Spirit's guidance is typically more intimate, more 'tactful', more empowering. When a married couple grow together, they can sense what each other is thinking. When two dancers, two trapeze artists, two people who play tennis as a double, weld into a single team, they don't need to call out the moves. If we grow in God's love, we will be more and more 'on the Spirit's wavelength' and, by a divine *instinct*, our reckonings will become sure.

Of course, ideas will 'come into our minds' while we read the Scriptures, pray, think, talk, relax, lie awake at night, and so on. The more we have been formed by the Scriptures, by the Church's Liturgy, by good preaching and teaching, and by practising the virtues, the better we can 'test the inspirations', as St John puts it. The more we love God, the more likely these ideas are to be sound. The less the Spirit will have to be like the wind that diverts us; the more He will be like the wind that fills our sails. It will not be a case of God acting *instead* of me, but of God acting so that *I act divinely*.

The Gift of Counsel the Spirit gives us enables us to appreciate Jesus' moral teaching. Some of what Jesus asks is asked of individuals. He asked a rich man to sell what he had, give to the poor, and join Jesus in His wandering ministry (*Mk* 10:21). Such requests have been called "counsels" ('advice') since they are not commands issued to everyone – Jesus told someone else *not* to follow Him in *that* way (*Mk* 5:18-19). But the rich man's journey to God was made much harder by his refusal of Jesus' request (*Mk* 10:22-25). It is very important that each one of us lets the Spirit guide him or her into the way of life Jesus requests.

Jesus does give a Law that is meant for everyone. He begins the Sermon on the Mount with the Eight

Beatitudes: "Blessed are the poor in spirit...Blessed are those who mourn... Blessed are the meek..." This Law is strange: it is not at all obvious that we are happier if we are poor or sad, put-upon or persecuted, desperately concerned about justice or truth, taken out of ourselves by helping others, or driven to wade into situations of conflict to promote reconciliation! But Jesus told us we *are* happiest if we are like that. By the Gift of Counsel the Holy Spirit gets us to see things Jesus' way, opening our eyes to see the strange beauty of His teaching.

Jesus did not mean that we *always* have to let ourselves be put upon. Sometimes we have to defend ourselves for the sake of those we are committed to. His Law is to be applied by a kind of mental agility – an agility granted and directed by the Holy Spirit.

The Spirit's advice, leading us to make right judgments here and now, includes helping us see our way through temptation. When we hear the word 'temptation' we tend to think of greed and lust, laziness and anger, and so on – the moral disorders within us. In the Bible, the word *peirazo*, to 'tempt', really means 'to try someone out' so as to reveal what is within them. Jesus was "put to the test in every respect as we are" (*Heb* 4:15), not because there was any moral disorder in Him – of course there was not – but because He was put under pressure by Satan, by His enemies, by the natural fear of pain and death, and by His friends. In all of this, He remained loyal to His Father's will.

Jesus was led by the Spirit when He began to face down temptation (*Lk* 4:1-13). In the Spirit He *knew* how to counter false advice. He was urged to turn stones into bread; later He was mobbed for miracles that impeded His preaching mission (*Mk* 1:35-38, 45). He had to focus on His ministry. We, too, who have limited time, must on occasion give up what is legitimate and good, for the sake of what is better. The Spirit helps us know what path to take.

Jesus was offered all the kingdoms of the world; His supporters wanted to take Him by force and make Him King (*Jn* 6:15); His close friend did not want Him to suffer (*Mt* 16:21-25). Instead, He chose the Way of the Cross so as to win a much deeper victory, and grant us a much greater freedom. The Spirit helps us *know how* to share His Sacrifice, imitate His self-giving love.

Jesus was tempted to throw Himself down from the pinnacle of the Temple; His enemies taunted Him to come down from the Cross and force them to believe (*Mt* 27:42). Instead He drew them by love (*Jn* 12:32). The Spirit helps us *know how,* in practical detail, to win people by love, by tact, by gentleness.

Insight into the beauty of the Faith

If we come to *understand* a subject really deeply, perhaps by studying it at university, we *become familiar with its basic principles*. These are what make it a single body of knowledge. We acquire a confidence in their truth, we appreciate their beauty and coherence. When we turn to the truths about God the Holy Trinity, and about how we may journey into God through the Passion and Resurrection of the incarnate Son, we cannot master this subject in the same way. "We walk by faith and not by sight" (2 *Co* 5:7). God *knows* Himself and His plan; the angels and Saints see Him and see into His plan. We rely on God to tell us about Himself and His offer; we trust Him to have done so truthfully. No matter how much theology we study, we must still grasp the truths of faith *by Faith*.

We can come to know that the world only exists because YHWH is 'making things to be'. We cannot yet *know by clear proof* that YHWH is the Holy Trinity. We remain 'out of our depth' when trying to demonstrate the coherence of all that He has revealed. Nevertheless, the Holy Spirit does give us an increasing sense of the beauty of what we believe. By the Gift of Understanding or Insight, He makes us able to sense, to feel, 'how right it all is'. Jesus has told us, as His friends, all He heard from His Father (*Jn* 15:15). The promised Spirit of Truth guides us, in love, to welcome the Father's Word, to ponder and penetrate it, respond to it and apply it (*Jn* 16:12-15).

We are made for truth and beauty, for friendship, for God. We can be brought to savour how we are called to abide within the Friendship that is God the Holy Trinity. We can be struck by the friendship by which God the Son became one of our family and laid down His life for us. We can appreciate the generosity by which Jesus remains with His friends in the Holy Eucharist. We cannot get our heads round *human* loyalty, though we rejoice in it. We should not expect to comprehend *God's* friendship as we can comprehend an academic subject. But the Holy Spirit can catch us up to rejoice in the friendship we have been shown. He can lead us to love God with all our *mind* (*Mk* 12:30), He can strengthen us to lay hold on the immensity of Christ's love which surpasses knowledge (*Ep* 3:16-19). By letting us glimpse the beauty of what God has shown us, He lets us glimpse its *truth*.

Knowing how to give an account of the hope that is in us

Suppose we have the Gift of Understanding, and are convinced of the rightness of the Catholic Faith. We can still find it difficult to cope with every challenge to our Faith. Someone sits next to you on a train journey, and asks you if you have read *The Da Vinci Code* or The *God Delusion*. You have until the next station to explain how these books do not disprove the Christian Faith! Or you listen to a debate on television or radio, and hear objections to the Faith that are new to you. How do you come to see that they do not hold water?

St Peter tells us to "be prepared to make a defence to anyone who calls you to account for the hope that is in you, yet do it with gentleness and reverence" (1 *P* 3:15). But we cannot spend *all* our time studying the Faith, we cannot anticipate *every* difficulty. So Jesus tells us not to be over-anxious about what we are to say – even when put on trial – for the Holy Spirit will teach us, at that moment, what to say (*Lk* 12:11-12). By the Gift of Knowledge He makes us receptive to His own eloquence, so that even if our words are awkward, humanly speaking, an echo of His divine authority will sound.

St John tells his fellow-Christians that they have all been anointed – have received the Holy Spirit – and all know (1 *Jn* 2:20, cf. 2:27). Some people, it seems, had joined the Church without ever really grasping the Christian Faith, and had left when they realised their own ideas about Jesus did not fit. But if we remain close to the Spirit who helps the Body of disciples understand what Jesus meant (*Jn* 14:26) we can tell what ideas are incompatible with the Faith, and not be beguiled by them.

"Until Christ be formed in you" – sharing God's Wisdom, God's perspective

The wise person has 'a sense of the whole'. St Paul likens himself to a wise *architect* (1 *Co* 3:10). Stonecarvers, brick-layers, carpenters, plumbers all do their bits – but the architect has the vision of how it must all fit together.

Greek culture prized Wisdom, *sophia*. It threw up many philosophers, lovers of wisdom. St Paul was rude about philosophy, for in his day it had degenerated into a rather mix-and-match affair, but the Church has always valued sound philosophy, the serious attempt to use human reason to see – as far as we can – 'how it all fits together'. The Church values sound theology, the reverent attempt to use God's revelation to see – still as far as we can – 'how it all fits together'. This too is a wisdom.

Of course there can be a 'worldly wisdom', a warped perspective that 'sees' how to turn everything to selfish advantage. St James slates this 'wisdom' in his Letter (3:14-16). By contrast, he says, the *Wisdom from Above* (i.e. from *God*) is pure and peaceable.

This Wisdom from above is not learned, not something accessible only to intellectuals. It is the greatest of the Seven Gifts of the Holy Spirit. In fact, it is St James' own cousin, Jesus Christ.

Wisdom in Scripture

In the Old Testament, Wisdom is with God as a beloved child and master craftsman (*Pr* 8:30), forming the world in all its beauty (*Pr* 8:22-31; *Si* 24:1-7; *Ws*

7:17-27). She offers her teaching – her bread and wine – generously (*Pr* 8:1-21, 8:32-9:16); she enters holy souls to make them friends of God (*Ws* 7:27); she "comes to abide" among God's People, especially in the form of the Law that guided them (*Si* 24:8-29). For the Jews, the Manna that fed God's People for their journey symbolised the Law that guided their way. The Books of Proverbs, Sirach and Wisdom celebrate the way in which Wisdom helps us see how everything fits together, and see in practical detail how to live out our role in family and society.

Jesus crucified is God's mysterious Wisdom (1 *Co* 1:23-24), who is always with God as His beloved Child, and through whom all things were made. He came to abide among us in the flesh to be the Way. He is the True Manna who nourishes us for our journey by giving His Body and Blood. The Eucharist, the Sacrament of His Sacrifice, forms us to imitate His self-giving. He abides within us. (See *Jn* 1:14, 6:32-35, 48-58, 14:6, 23, 15:1-14; 1 *Co* 11:23-33).

Jesus did not only utter the Eight Beatitudes, He lived them out and died by them; we must imitate Him. So, St James says (3:17), the Wisdom from God is pure, peaceable, fair, obedient, full of mercy and good fruits, non-judgmental, not hypocritical. Divine Wisdom is marked by the spirit of the Beatitudes and of the Seven

Gifts. In particular, St Thomas suggests (*Tertia Pars* 45, 6) Wisdom goes with "Blessed are the peacemakers, for they shall be called sons of God" (*Mt* 5:9). We are called to share the sonship of Jesus, the Divine Wisdom (*Jn* 1:12; *Rm* 8:14-17; 1 *Jn* 3:1-2), called to share the mind of Christ (*Ph* 2:5). He came to be and to make peace (*Is* 9:6-7; *Ep* 2:13-22; *Col* 1:20), and if we share His mind we will make peace (*Ph* 2:1-5).

Sharing the mind of Christ

For if we share the mind of Christ, if we are conformed to the Divine Wisdom, *we share God's perspective on things.* We see everything, everyone, ourselves, *in the light of God.* And so we can tell what really matters. And what doesn't.

For example, suppose you and your brother inherit some money. He manages to get his hands on the whole of it, leaving you with none. Maybe you have a duty to contest this, and claim back money that you and your dependants need. But maybe the Holy Spirit will lead you to 'turn the other cheek'. Maybe, in Wisdom, you will see that the money – which lasts for a time – doesn't really matter. Peace, which lasts for ever, does. The Spirit, who is equal to the Father, brings us to maturity by teaching us a divine Wisdom so that, in all sorts of practical ways, we can make sure judgments according to the mind of Christ (1 *Co* 2:6-16).

Wisdom and Charity go together; they reinforce each other. For if, by Wisdom, we see ourselves and others from God's point of view, we will share God's love for ourselves and them, God's thirst for our and their true good. If by Charity we share God's delight in ourselves and others, we will share His vision for ourselves and them.

If we are true friends with someone, we are on her wavelength, we naturally share her perspectives. She points out to us things and people she is interested in; we see them with her eyes. By Charity, Father, Son and Spirit are our Friends; the Spirit stands by us to point people out to us and speak to us of His project for them, and by Wisdom we can see them with His eyes.

When God the Father sends His Son and Their Spirit, the Son and the Spirit also bring each other. Jesus is conceived in Mary's womb by the power of the Holy Spirit, and breathes the Spirit on us, His disciples. The Spirit is called down to make the bread and wine become Christ's Body and Blood, and we who are nourished by that Body and Blood are filled with the Holy Spirit.

Father, Son and Spirit want to *give Themselves to us*, to be known and loved, possessed and enjoyed, now and for ever (St Thomas, *Prima Pars* 43). In particular, the Father sends Son and Spirit to abide within us. When the Son, the Divine Wisdom, comes, we are formed in Wisdom. When the Spirit, the Divine Love, comes, we are formed in Love. They bring each other: Wisdom is a

Gift of the Holy Spirit, and the Divine Wisdom, dwelling within us, breathes forth Love.

Come Holy Spirit

Come, O Holy Spirit, fill the hearts of your faithful People,
and enkindle in them the fire of your love.

Send forth your Spirit, that they may be created;
And so renew the face of the earth.

Let us pray.
O God, you have taught the hearts of your faithful People by the light of the Holy Spirit.
Give us, then, the same Spirit to make us truly wise,
and grant us always to know the joy of his counsel,
through Christ our Lord. Amen.

By making us divinely wise, the Spirit "brings Christ to birth" in us. This starts in Baptism, when the Spirit brings us to birth as God's beloved children, and in Confirmation, when He brings us to maturity. He 'Christens' us, makes us Jesus' members, forms us into Christ. But our 'coming to birth' is a labour that will only be complete at the final resurrection (*Rm* 8:18-25). It involves a continuous conversion as we take Jesus' mentality on board. So St Paul felt himself to be in labour with his flock "until Christ be formed in you" (*Ga* 4:19).

Confirmation – sharing Jesus' ministry and glory

In Confirmation, we are 'brought to maturity'. However, it's a strange kind of maturity! Like reaching adulthood, or like being promoted to a new job – but even more so – this maturity is a *gift* and *project* that *comes upon us*. I was given it at the age of 9. In the Eastern Churches it is given to babies. Confirmation empowers us to *start* undertaking the responsibility of being mature in Christ. The spiritual gifts enable us to *grow up into Christ*, as St Paul puts it in *Ep* 4:12-16.

Maturity

The Seven Gifts are a key part of Christian moral maturity. Young children tend to follow adults' rules in a stiff way; teenagers sometimes rebel against them. When we are mature we see the value of the rules, and are wise enough to interpret and apply them as they are meant to be interpreted and applied. We can also take responsibility for demanding and awkward decisions.

That kind of maturity comes to us in Confirmation, though we may still have to learn to use it. We have seen how the Seven Gifts enable the flexible responsiveness we need if we are to live out our responsibilities as adult Christians. Hence the Spirit of the Seven Gifts is called down on us at Confirmation.

We have also seen that Christian maturity is quite the opposite of lonely, self-sufficient independence. Jesus tells us to become like little children (*Mt* 18:3-4, cf. *Mk* 10:15). To be mature in Christ means to be like Jesus, the Beloved Child, who was totally dependent on and devoted to His Father. The mature confidence given us in Confirmation is the confidence of being attuned to God's ways through the Spirit's guidance, not the brittle confidence of "going our own way". Confirmation commits us to a share in Jesus' public ministry in which He was "led by the Spirit" both more powerfully and more gently than we can be. We must accept the same Spirit's friendship.

So it's not just that we finish *growing* into Christ when the Spirit raises us from the dead (*Rm* 8:11). Our *coming to birth* is only completed then! We need, with St Thérèse of Lisieux, to recognise our ongoing 'spiritual infancy'.

The Sacrament

After all, Confirmation is a *Sacrament*. A Sacrament makes it clear that we are still on pilgrimage: God comes to us, but in such a way that we do not see Him and His work plainly. It points us back to Jesus' ministry and Sacrifice, it brings us the Spirit His Sacrifice channels to us, it points us forward to the coming Kingdom:

> Pour into it the strength of the Holy Spirit, by the cooperating power of your Christ, from whose holy Name this Chrism takes its name... Filled with royal, priestly and prophetic honour through this Sacrament you have established, may they be clothed with the garment of an incorrupt office. So may [this oil] be, for those who will have been reborn of water and the Holy Spirit, a saving Chrism; may it make them sharers in eternal life and heirs of heavenly glory.
>
> (Prayer for Consecrating Chrism, first option, translated very 'literally').

In Confirmation, God's new claim on us 'stamps' us permanently, puts a new quality in us, which is nothing less than a sharing in Jesus' own dignity as Prophet, Priest, and King. Chrism is a kind of royal and priestly robe which will last for ever. It expresses the radiance the anointing Spirit gives us now, as He makes us able as prophets to speak Christ's truth and love. It points to the glory the Spirit will give us when He raises us from the dead.

By the Seven Gifts, the Spirit guides us in the way of

the Beatitudes. He leads us to live now by the values of the City of God, where all the saved will be open to each other, rejoicing in each other's glory without envy. He conforms us to Christ, who came not to be served but to serve (*Mk* 10:45). He draws us to reflect our Father's mercy (*Lk* 6:35-36). Our heavenly Wisdom, our closeness to Jesus, our imitation of the Father, our friendship with the Spirit – in short, the Seven Gifts animated by Love – will reach their perfection when we abide together in God our Goal.

Wisdom is the nearest thing we have, now, to the Vision of God that will be our bliss then. While we walk by Faith, Wisdom is an instinct, a sense, a taste, a feel for the things of God – but also *a divine perspective on things*. The Wisdom who shares with us His Father's perspective on things, will in Heaven show us His Father. Then we shall see everything in the light of God, more clearly than we now can. Now we embrace the Father by Wisdom and Love; then we shall embrace Him by Vision and Love.

A prayer to the Holy Spirit (composed by Cardinal Manning)

O Holy Spirit of God, take us as your disciples.
Guide us, enlighten us, sanctify us.
Bind our hands that they may do no evil.
Cover our eyes that they may see it no more.
Sanctify our hearts that evil may not dwell within us.
Be our God and our Guide.
Wherever you lead us, we will go.
Whatever you forbid us we will renounce.
And whatever you command us, in your strength, we will do.
Lead us, then, into the fulness of your truth.

8 Deadly Sins

The Church has settled on a list of 7 mortal sins but the Fathers of the Church more often referred to 8. The deadly or capital sins - covetousness, envy, sloth, gluttony, lust, anger, vainglory and pride - are the most significant and insidious temptations with which we must contend. A first step in countering their influence is understanding their psychological and spiritual roots in human experience. Standing humbly in the truth about ourselves, we will appreciate the power of God's love to heal and strengthen our nature, for love is not jealous or boastful, not arrogant or rude, not irritable or resentful.

Vivian Boland, OP is Master of Students for the English Dominicans, lectures in theology at St Mary's, Twickenham and Blackfriars, Oxford. He also preaches retreats, and writes on theology and spirituality.

ISBN: 1 86082 460 9

CTS Code: SP 21

Spiritual Warfare

Every Christian is engaged in an ongoing struggle against the self, and against temptation, striving to gain the blessings of the Kingdom of God. This booklet enlightens the struggle by searching the wisdom of the scriptures. It gives hope to everyone, because Christ is always by our side to help us in every battle, and he has already defeated death and sin.

Vivian Boland, OP is Master of Students for the English Dominicans, lectures in theology at St Mary's, Twickenham and Blackfriars, Oxford. He also preaches retreats, and writes on theology and spirituality.

ISBN: 1 86082 421 0

CTS Code: SP 16